SOFT LAUNCH

James Dunn

B is For Beans #1

Bootstrap Press / Pressed Wafer
Lowell, MA / Boston, MA

First published in 2008.

Bootstrap Productions   Pressed Wafer
82 Wyman Street   9 Columbus Square
Lowell, MA 01852   Boston, MA 02116

Cover photograph by Derek Fenner.

Printed and bound in the US.
Distributed to the trade by Small Press Distribution.

ISBN 978-0-9779975-8-9

The author would like to thank the editors of the following *Can We Have Our Ball Back*, *Meanie*, *EOAGH*, *Only the Blind See this World*, and *The East Village* where some of these poems appeared.

This publication was made possible by donations to Bootstrap Productions, Inc. and Pressed Wafer. Consider helping us support contemporary arts and literary culture.

THIS IS A BOOTSTRAP PRESSED WAFER PRODUCTION!

for Gerrit,
Angela, Seamus & Gavin

CONTENTS

CATHEDRALS OF TIME

IN PLAIN AIR

BEYOND BURNT BRIDGES

THE PATRON SAINTS BEHIND THE GREEN DOOR

Cathedrals of Time

MY FORGOTTEN REVOLVER

In the empty chambers
Of my forgotten revolver,
A nervous finger twitches
Sunday pigeons take to air

This sensible century screams
A final pauper's prayer
To the inebriated angels
Swigging the clouds
Losing their laughter

REMAINS OF THE CITY

He himself was ruins –
miles of memory
along devastated silences

He remains of the city;
An armed Venus
Wrapping his mind
Around Beacon Hill

Remains of the city
Of great harbor fog-
Harbor of bricked building gray gloom
Arctic cold wind
blasting down Devonshire

The shadowed scurry of rats
Across the Common
Between the gnarled roots
Of trees in front of
The golden domed Capitol
Near the fountain of youthful odes
Singing sweet the soft syllables from God

Sick and suffering, the afflicted
Ebb and flow into Mass General
As your silent patient ghost
Sits shrouded in the lobby
Waiting for the male nurse
To come down with your check

The Old Charles Prison
Stone gray cathedral of time
With pigeons for eyes
Blanched droppings
For tears -
Where Anthony DeSalvo

Bragged of his crimes-
Transformed into a boutique hotel

The familiar is foreign to me
And hardened with sad empty
    Conjurings
In the Harvard Gardens history
a glass of whiskey

Where sat three poets
Reading the rain on the window
Now sits one man alone
Trying to tell a girl what
Remains of the city
Is ruins without you

POEM FOR ED WORD

Your eyes are arbitrary
Fuzzy dice
Rolling snake eyes
One from one

Your hair is frazzled hieroglyphics
Written above a winter coat

Your hands are secret histories
Never to be told
Your open palms
Feed the ancient forest deer

Your voice is a rubber band clown
Wrapped around this snowy street
People populate with their late intentions.

MATTER OF WHEN

It's just the matter
Taken into impatient hands
Shaped into things to come
The moment is always here
A shadow chained to infinite crosses
The cat waits
And only acts when
He has become nothing
The clouds clash in their gray armor
Lightning is midwife
The storm is born
In a bag of ragged winds
To the bright leaves
Wet on their way down
To the dirt of the graves
The earth holds in her molten womb

POEM FOR JACK MICHELINE

I want to make love to yr parked blue buick in the dull
 driveway
I want to dance the osmosis blues all over yr sloppy silence
I want to slip you something made of fascist manifestos and
 extravagant drapery
I want to inhale yr warm laundry in the dimly lit laundromat
 where you fold yr sorrows
I want to pummel yr smile with petunias planted in barbed
 wire
I want to shimmer like a distant visitor in a government
 passport application line in the Tip O'Neil building
I want to please the crowd that never showed up at the party I
 never threw
I want to grip a monkey like he was made of milkshakes
I want to drop in on a mandolin and pluck the strings from the
 jaws of disaster
I want to tease the gleaming shattered glass flashing Morse
 code kisses to the lonely housewife in the sun
I want to sample the snores of the world with an open mouth
 and a windpipe in my hand
I want to stroke the genius that runs along the hem of your
 crushed velvet couch
I want to lick every James Dean postage stamp you wiped yr
 brow with
I want to lambada to the top of the Bunker Hill monument
 and throw confetti tears from its gentle portal upon the
 sleeping history of Charlestown
I want to chime to the ceiling the depths of my cherry soda
 sorrows
I want to charm the determined snakes dancing on the burning
 sand of yr brown belly
I want to hitch hike to my bedroom and get a hummer in the
 Molly Pitcher rest area by a hooker dressed as a Hessian
I want to find the blackened match that Sherman dropped in
 Atlanta and that Muhammad Ali raised to the sky

I want to jump the turnstiles that spin their surprise in yr eyes
like cabana ceiling fans
I want to wear a hard hat and a tool belt to my First
Communion
I want to repair the headlights on the speeding late model
sedan that zooms through yr dinner hour
I want to tip-toe around the unmentioned package tucked
under yr arm
I want to rivet the onlookers with bull frogs that claim to be
questions
I want to blare from yr speakers the gospels of St Genet as
enemy aircraft drop condolences
I want to outdistance the picket fence that marches after
midnight and the lonely seminarian who slowly opens a jar
I want to slurp yr sweet and sour soup and gargle with the
gargoyles in yr closet
I want to feel the same premonition the conductor felt as he
slowed yr train to an emergency stop
I want to color the caravan charcoal diamond moonlight and
number the sands in yr name

OCEANS OF MY HEAD

Estimating the weight
of these golden shackles,
Doped to the gills
With gravity's inertial charm,

I sit back
upon the centuries
And swim through
The oceans of my head.

Somewhere else,
light bulbs burn out.

Somewhere else,
A bell rings true

TIGHT QUARTERS

Living close together
brings new meaning
To holiday cheer.

Lost in momentary haze
of a whipped cream whippet
household sounds echo eternal,
for a briefed inhaled moment;
a persistence of ricochets
down the corridor of holiday dreams

Drowning flaming boiled eggs
with Irish whiskey,
at the B-Side lounge

Walked to the house
of a thousand felines
to see a man in a tattered robe
about a beer wagon Clydesdale.

Another cold one down
Receiving secret codes
in a cat house on Christmas day.

A dusky drive along Route 99
through the heart of sleeping Malden,
everything unwrapping.
The blinking lights illuminate
empty snowy streets
in the Christmas quiet.

SWEET SUDDEN ORCHESTRAL SILENCE

The dance is a shadow
On walls that rise

The sound is a sunrise
That shadows the moon

Here's where the strings
Break your heart

Blue wanderings in
Undreamt rooms
Lights are real
In orange darkness

Slight open hand
Balloons
Bobble in
Parking lot
Winds

Fracture in
The foundation
And all
Things frayed
Begin
To heal

THE FLIGHT OF STAIRS
for John Wieners 1/6/99

Who will come after you
        up the creaking stairs
Catching your spilt breath
        between eternal sighs?

Ticker tape parade
        of fragmented memories
Shards of pure hope
        blue fire in your West Coast eyes

Shadows of collages
        peeling from your apartment wall
A dress shirt on a hanger
        fluttering in an open window
                in the trinity of rooms

Ghosts of your heaven
        furnish your forty-four joys with belief

Ghosts of your heaven
        dancing in the whispering traffic
                on the bohemian side of Beacon Hill

Steve Jonas' invisible twin
        conducting street-peopled symphonies
                with a lit cigarette baton

Ghost of your heaven—
        the wicker butterfly
                on the adjacent door of apartment nine

Your East Coast ocean eyes
        rain their flooded blue streets down

Yeah, or yes, rather---
   the number ten shines in gold

Through the crack
   I count the broken stars
     in your eyes
as I turn away towards
   the flight of stairs

THE HALLUCINOGENIC TOREADOR

Gala is Christ's sad angelic face on
The shroud of Turin in the corner
The armless statues make his face
The gadflies fly towards the boy
The bull bleeds a puddle of resort lake
With a club med girl rafting on the blue blood
Voltaire is the two maids pouring jugs of water
The dalmation is reduced to its spots
The bull's mortal wound is a matrix of rainbow dots
The 5 dances on the face of venus
It is the magic hour for the dance of killing the bull
Left breast is his nose
Belly is his mouth
Turned upward to the right
The green tie
The buttoned top button
The rose on the red cape draped over his shoulder
Sailor boy holds his bone
Like a firehose in the hands of a pyro

DEATH IS A STRANGE HIGHWAY MARKER

Alive in quiet silent
Invisible ways now
Living in my head
Visiting in my dreams
Sadly beautiful light
Of visionary days when
You are so real in
Manner and speaking
The verbal shorthand
Of a memory or visitor
Who has left days before
In advance of us to
Move beyond time
And to mark time
Painfully for those
Still under rule of
The wounded clocks
That go around in
A show of hands
In askance for to be
Held is to behold
The beauty that brings
Its own balance of heart
Desire for an empty chair
For one more moment
With the one who rocked
Endlessly upon it
Swirling thoughts around
The room like a fractured
Carousel with fairies
Riding wooden winged
Horses galloping upon
A brass pole like a stripper
On Christmas eve outside
The Navy base gates
A prayer that circles like

Smoke and trails off
Into empty promises
The early morning
Rolling thunder
Speaking truth
Is just jets breaking
Sound barriers in
The cold New England
Frosty morning quiet
The prison yard out back
Bricked to be walled in
Where children dance
Upon cement pastures
And unfettered futures.

PLASTIC

Plastic is anything we ask it to be
If we asked it to be time it would
Plastic makes everything possible
If only we could melt into puddles

Plastic connects the world, the forest to the trees
Water rolls off the shining leaves in unfurling furies
Nine plastic sisters admire the Tupperware god
Contain us in this form – form us in this container

Plastic toys with the divinity of creation
Halos for beer cans—death muzzles for wishing whales
An artificial bond between water and it's captor, the
    bucket, or,
The lone shopping bag puffed full of wind in a bare winter
    tree.

Plastic zip locks leftover lives
The fruits of the marble juicy tree (Violence is for men
who learn to know)

Plastic laughs like a soldier at the wax figures on fire
In the amazing museum torched by false treaties.

Plastic tell us who we will become
If we asked it to be God
It would
Take his shape

In Plain Air

RAINBAUD

Ashen as he was
I saw a child dancing in his eyes
In the solitary star of the night sky
So fondly, we dream

Broken by beauty's abyss on the other side
Where our desire can never be satisfied
The fractured heart spits out crippled blood
The wants of the soul whip the crack of lust

Shine a lipstick flashlight down the aquarium
Corridors of lost saints
As they deny the dirt of their bodies
For the saliva of salvation drooling from heaven

Let US sing the praises of the subversive
Moralist who stops his bleeding
By opening more veins

The color red is the tears of the rainbow
Black is the melodrama of minstrels
Yellow is a halogen halo on a horny hobo
Purple is the regal tourniquet of champions
Orange is the anniversary of an execution
White is the moaning bed sheets of morning
Indigo is the anthropology of blood spit into the ground
Tan is the earth of the flesh warmed by hymns to a soldier
Gold is the peace of sleeping orphans with an airplane
     passing overhead
Silver is the beard of the clouds stroked by the great
     greasepaint ghost

The rainbow is Rimbaud
(The rainbow is Rilke
Rilke is the row boat
The row boat is Baudelaire

Baudelaire is the dancing bear
The dancing bear is Genet
Genet is the cloud ceiling
The cloud ceiling is the clairvoyant
The clairvoyant is Rimbaud)
Rimbaud is the rainbow

OPEN FIRE

Three poets visited
in my dreams

One, dead.

Two, very much
Beyond the reaches
Of sound

One had eyes
That danced like
Puppet clowns

He whispered
These words
As a spiritual aside
On a British terrace

"Less words in
the poem

Less poems
in the book.

Free
The poem."

One had the
 Sunshine smile
Of a secret saint

It was on a double
Decker tour bus
En plein air

He turned slowly
Into the downtown
wind
of the metroplis city
saying,
You
Are my most
Cherished admirer

The third stepped away
From the clamoring crowd
At a reading at Emerson Hall
Where Ralph Waldo sits bronze
And frozen with his considerable
Nose in the Harvard air.

From the podium, he turned
And looked me in the eye
With his one good one
And said,
"Arm your words
with kindness,
and open fire."

A PUNCH IS A POEM

A punch is a poem written in distress
With the rhythm of violence, and
The beauty of a brutal beating

The white light of pain flashes
Angels in waiting
Falling from the aftershock
of consciousness lost

The lightning crack of a fist is
A sonnet written with bruised knuckles
The head snaps back in slow motion
As the music of muscles plays on the pipes
Of a disfigured dream.

A punch is a poem in protest unwritten
A shout caught in your shoe
A hemorrhage of sad stars
A roman candle of despair
Going off in your hands

A poem is a gob of spit
Armed with a hammer
Ramming the sky
With a thousand evil anvils

A punch is an apology
Delivered in a pipe bomb

A poem is hope returned
For insufficient postage

A poem is a punch
Gunning for God
Hoping to land
Square on the jaw.

AMERICAN OCEANS

American Oceans broken
With violent claps in the waves
Lighting up with the green blue
Glow of phosphorescent wonder
Spreading across the shore like
A blanket of foamy fingers. The
American Ocean sprays the lonely
Highways of dusk. In these waters the
Drowning is patriotic and the
Swimming becomes sleep.

A century of whitecaps break in the
History of fair winds and the time
Honored tradition of following seas.
American Ocean of thee I drink until
My lungs are filled with your salt.
American Oceans, I open my eyes
Under your water and the green dream
Invites me to scream in hieroglyphic bubbles.
A lonely island waits patiently to greet me.
The American Ocean washes me ashore
Under the Statue of Liberty's dress.

I swim with the fishes with a concrete heart.
I saw the Longfellow bridge announce the
Apocolypse. I floated by Plum Island with
A shark cage in my head. I freestyled
To the Vineyard with leisure on my mind.
American Oceans coax tossing tiny ships
Into sweetly sinking. American Oceans
Flood the world with her blue cars and
Her green tides. American Notions
American Oceans

The sun paints the shadowy sunken ship's blue
Underbelly. Heralding a new time

and ushering in the drowning century.
Baiting our breath in
The vast rocky waters of the American Ocean.
Seagulls spread their laughter in Pacific time,
Turning their wings to sing sudden surprises to
The muted morning. Under the whirl of water
An anchor sinks for her mistress,
Her algae covered belly
Her soft submerged cleft shrouded in seaweed.
American Notion, the great national sea side
Thought bubble trailing towards the humble sky
The depths of the empty sorrows, chilled
Murky green towards the unending floor.

A BOUQUET OF BRUISES

The lilacs luck out in the lukewarmth
of your soothing sins-
A beehive and a chained devil-
an anchor and a bouquet of bruises

Throw your head back into the night sky
Stunned to secret tears at the sinister
Beauty of the bell tower.

Traveling along the ridge between two worlds
In your convertible silence.
Unspoken intentions are buried burdens
Beneath our breath

I found my voice
In the ricochet of your words
I dreamed your moans
Married my ears

I awoke to the sound of empty bells
Through the cracks in the dawn

ANGEL OF MY MISTAKES

for Angela

You are the angel of my mistakes
Watching over me in sad caution
Smiling achingly towards the world
Wings beating the rhythm of dreams
Green eyes reflecting like sunflowers
Afloat down a winding stream

You are the angel of my misfortune
Taking me in your flight
And keeping me from myself

Smiling achingly towards the world
Wings beating the rhythm of dreams
Your soft warm skin is mad beautiful music
The ache of your soul the beating of rain
On a lonely afternoon rooftop
The sound of an airplane in the distance
Is your muted cry to be touched once again.

KILL DRIFTER

Kill drifter
To sustain erection
In the empty desert
Of the soul

Walk miles
To quell restlessness
In the simmering skillet
Of the mind

Drink venom
To nourish the demons
In the holy haunts
Of the flesh

Calm nerves
To hear the beating
In the corridors
Of a caged heart

Taste Eternity
To see golden shadows
In the shattered
ruins of the day

FATHER OF NIGHT

Clouds so swift,
they roll and kiss
forming a perfect
smoky sculpture
of my father on his deathbed.
Out to sea, miles off
the coast of Gloucester
I see his slack
jawed open mouth
robbed of speech,
without a vocabulary.

Each breath a lifetime
of forgotten childhoods
An eyebrow raised
formed by the shadows
The pained expression
in roiling white plumes

Out of the water,
into the sky on a string,
a dying haddock lands
at the end of his fight,
gaffed and mouthing a kiss –
sad desperate O's,
just to try to breathe again.

Outside

The blue sea water
as he flops on the deck.

Twice I've felt
the spirit of a man
dying pass directly
through me;

once, my ear to his lips
awaiting a secret
or a final kiss.
The other, my hand
on his heart
as it fluttered as wings
on a trapped thing,
then ceased to beat.
The sad broken bagpipe
exhale of the last breath
so intimate in my ear
and slow to end
an ocean wind whistling
through the attics
of winter.

Beyond Burnt Bridges

IT IS TRUE

I've spent my dues
Left too many clues
Broke the truce
Danced like a noose
Pissed in the juice

It is possible

I gave you false hope
Burnt yr heart with a rodeo rope
Made you drop the soap
Blew white smoke at the pope
Kissed yr voluptuous cantaloupe

It is likely

I ran out on the bill
Filled my cup to spill
Covered yr whispers with clean fill
Set the values to permanent nil
Stole a thrill in a car speeding over a hill

It is feasible

I crumpled yr soul
Wrinkled yr secret button hole
Shopped for excuses in a store for the large and tall
Rented a room in the attic of a doll
Flooded yr phone booth with prank collect calls
Blessed yr stalls with the glory of holes

It is viable

I streamed yr windshield with tears
Plied your guardian angel with beers
Prepared to pay for those gears

Quilted yr dreams into fears

It is reasonable

I punctuated the sidewalk with ampersands
Drank the dirty water from hot dog stands
Put on my shoes without first making plans
Went to school with swollen glands
Blessed my children with the names of brands

It is possible

I chiseled an escape
Served High Mass dressed only in a cape
Sat against plexiglass with a sad lonely ape
Stole from shadows their shape
Played with myself and screamed rape
Drank a fifth of scotch tape

It is true

FOR WATER TO RUN
A Poem For Children Who Lack Self Control

For water to run, it must have sea legs
When it tires it forms a pool
For a madman to crack, he must have three eggs
Unless the chickens deem him a fool.

For whistles to cry, they must shed tears
That roll down the cheek of the sky
For sirens to wail, they must harbor fears
Flashing red in their mad blinking eye.

For dogs to hunt, they must have tender prey,
Or, the scent of an escapee's trail.
For horses to spook, they must sense the ghost in the hay,
And wish the flies away with their tail.

For thunder to clap, it must have two hands
Or, one hand striking God's face
For cows to come home, you must meet their demands
And lead them back home to their place.

For angels to sing, they must have pure voices
That cascade from the heavens above
For bees to sting, they must hear certain noises
Like bells, or the cooing of doves.

For sparks to fly, they must have wings of flame
So in flight they burn down the night
For clouds to gather, they call each other by name
Forging their shape into a divine beard of white.

For flames to dance, they must taste the heat
That chortles in orange and blue
For crowds to roar, lions must be thrown at their feet
Where mild mannered madmen are martyred on cue.

For roads to wind, they must have dangerous curves
And striped lines that warn of demise
For buildings to stand, they must have steel nerves
And blue sky in the windows of their eyes.

For stars to shine, they must be polished by night
So, like jewels they capture the light
For cats to hiss, they must slowly leak fright
Like a tire kissing a nail goodnight.

BATTLES LOST

Edward Redfield stood in front
of the Center Bridge in Solebury, Pa.
From the same spot years earlier,
he watched the original
Bridge to New Jersey
burn down from a lightning strike.

The day after the bridge fire,
he painted
for hours waist deep in snow
The only painting
he would ever paint from memory.

He believed
To paint cold
you must be cold.

He started his own fire
in front of the bridge
He casually tossed several
paintings into the flames
watching tenderly as each one
was consumed by the fire.

His only reason—
These paintings are battles lost.

I CARRY YOU

I carry you
    With me in my heart

You are dead weight
    Under the grass whispers

But inside, I carry you like
    A secret that got drunk and told

Alive with those winter blue sighs
    It's nice to see you blowing smoke

I carry you
    Untold distances in my heart

How I cried,
    When you dried up in my mind

How your evening imploded
    With a flowering rose of memories

There are thorns never to be found
    In the buried crown of flowers

I carry you
    Through the streets that paved over yr name

There is no measure
    Or rhythm to the silence you left for me

Your words randomly written for other
    Lovers and visions, lifetimes and vacancies

There's a monstrous trembling
    That's yet to arrive, an earthquake yet to be born

I carry you
  With me

You are light-headed
 in my heart

JELLY DONUT

Today, I am not an American
nor a citizen of the world.

Today, I am a man divided.
Today, I am a man multiplied.

Today, I am a jelly donut.

A city multiplied is the reciprocal
of man divided equal to
the square root of infinity's trees.

Today, I am a jelly donut.

A city divided multiplied by man
who carries the one
is less than equality.

A man divided multiplied by the city
over the one
is greater than insanity.

Yesterday, I was a cup of coffee.
Tomorrow, I'll be toast.

Yesterday, I was a zebra prison.
Tomorrow, I will be a well dressed lunch.

Today, I am a man multiplied.
Today, I am a city divided.

Today, I am a jelly donut.

EDICT TO THE SHADOWS

You must not hide from
The endangered day any longer
Like a frenzy of bats huddled
Together in mysterious shapes of night

You must come out
From yourself
Dissolve into melting mirages
Of vanished jewelry

Dance alone
On the highway
To the whims of the wind
Moving memories
Roaming clouds
Sentence you to dusk.

A POEM FOR THE GREAT WALLENDA

Life is on the wire
Everything else is
Just waiting

God was with me
On the falling pyramid
As my family crashed
Upon me in such
Colossal collapse

God was with me
At Tallulah Gorge
Where I stood
On my head with the
Wind blowing stronger
Than I had planned.

A picture in my pocket
As I whispered over again
God is with me

God was with me at
Veteran's stadium
On opening day, 1971
I tip-toed across the sky
And dropped the first ball
Of the season into
Tim McCarver's mitt, as
All eyes held their breath.

God was with me
In San Juan
His warm breath
Was in the wind
It made me drunk
With a tremulous

Teetering

I knew it had to be
I could have grabbed
The rope on my way down

But, life was on the wire
And gravity conspired
With the wind as
I came crashing down
On the bumper of a parked car

I had perfected my last trick
Everything else was just waiting

INVOCATION FROM A BUNKER

Bullet
Shatter my window

Intruder
Break down my door

Redemption
Fall from the ceiling

Salvation
Rise through the floor

The Patron Saints Behind the Green Door

A SERIES OF COATS

July 22nd

Friday Saints
Be praised
On the Feast
Of St Mary Magdalene
Patroness of
repentant prostitutes

A woman's chastity
Consists of
A series of coats
Like an onion,
Said Hawthorne

Like an onion,
A series of ghosts,
That hang in the air
A chaste woman
Is never caught
With her coat off

She's a blowen,
A bloom, a blossom,
A woman without special
Reference to moral character
A showy courtesan
Among the criminal classes
An American mistress

I have one last one
And then someone
Else will have to
Step into my shoes
Against the faces,
the forces, rather,

of doom

The next scene
would be Marc
Anthony's tent

THE COUVADE

July 25th

THE FEAST EVE OF ST ANNE

Wearing a peach dress
She cradled her baby
A note pinned to her bra
Another on the table
Begging forgiveness

28 floors/one landing
On the Seventh
The thud followed the scream
Residents thought a great bird
Large and shadowy swooped
Past their panoramic view of
The Boston Harbor on a summer day

Her husband came home in time
To see them take flight from
The open window in the Devonshire
His blank dismayed face stared from
The stretcher as the ambulance
Took him to Mass General
Where he remained under
Heavy sedation.

The strength of limit
The limited degree of strength
It is customary for women
To acquire before they suffer
To go abroad after child bearing

Patroness of fertility and birthing
Peculiar post-partum tradition

Practiced by South American Indians

The *couvade* – the man-bed
The father rests in bed/is well nourished/
Receives congratulatory visits
While the wife immediately goes
Back to her household duties
Immediately after birth.

Elsewhere it is believed
The wife's ailments are
Borne by the husband
Who endures neuralgia
And morning sickness
In place of the mother.

UNDER THE ROSE

September 3rd

THE FEAST OF ST. ROSE

Under the rose
Sub rosa
In secret

Cupid offered
The rose
To Harpocrates
The god of silence
To remain quiet
About Venus'
Amorous discretions.

In Tudor times
Banquet halls
Were decorated
With painted roses

Women wore garlands
Of roses to remind
The revelers

Anything said or done
Under the influence

Would remain
Under the rose

GROUND SQUIRRELS

Stoopers hunt around
The debris at racetracks
For winning stubs not cashed in
"outs," thrown down by mistake,
Ripped apart in unreasoned rage.

Some tickets require
Great skill and patience
To be fitted together again
From the confetti of frustrations.

Amateur stoopers wander
Around grandstands
Picking up discarded
Tote tickets in the hope
They will find a live one.

Professional stoopers
ground squirrels
Train their eyes
On the forgotten floor.

TAKE A FLOURISH

Enjoy a woman
In a hasty manner

Take a flyer
With clothes on
Not in bed

Colonial politician
William Byrd
Favored "roger"
Over flourish
With vigor
Not withstanding
she was indisposed

 Adding sport
To carnal pleasures

Rogered my wife
But forgot to say
My prayers

MUSTARD SHINE

Mustard on the shoes
Of prison escapees

Throws the bloodhounds
Off the trail of their scent

A little mustard oil
Olive oil and mustard
Or water and mustard

Applied after the
Trail has been scented

Renders bloodhounds
Powerless

Belief among thieves -
Superstition no less
Than honest men.

Very unlucky to
Steal a pack of cards

Equally unlucky
To rob a hunchback
Or a cripple

The most dangerous
Act of all is to
Rob a church
Particularly if a
Chalice is involved.

SOFT LAUNCH

the babies and the persistent ghosts,
the almost fingerprint forgotten faces,
the striking of a match cupped in an elegant hand,

the holy sound of distant traffic,
the downward slope of sunlight through the fluttering
    white curtains,
the fractures of the heart,
the distance between shadows and silhouettes,

the echo of the last ring of an ebony phone in the back
    room unanswered,
the slow procession of daylight down the morning covered
    hillside,
the dance down the supermarket aisle with goods in hand,
the gray Whitman beard shaved from a dead man's face,

the cigarette burning red embers of desire,
the maniacal martyrs in armored cars,
the prophet whose tongue is a torch for the future,
the flashing yellow of sleeping traffic lights,

the time and material of desperate acceptance,
the gentle reflection of passing clouds in pothole rain
    puddles,
the unfurling breath of the wind frosting the bedroom
    windows,
the needlework of knitted doom,

a soft launch

SLEEPWALKER

I sit silently upon
    the unmade bed
counting the footsteps
    echoing in the hallway.

The night wrecks me
    with certain torture
  that never
      ends.

Will I ever see ocean diamonds
    through these busted chains of the sea?

The green door
    unlocks its secrets
The sacred vision
    exploding orange roses
      blooming in your blue sleep.